Gift to the Present

Wellderly Wisdom

Maryann Glasgow
"Annie"

special thanks to Bil Keane
and Dale Anderson, M.D.

Beaver's Pond Press, Inc.
Edina, Minnesota

You are a Gift to the World!

Warmly,

Annie Glasgow

Family Circus cartoon © Bil Keane. Used by permission.

ISBN 1-931646-25-2

Library of Congress Catalog Number: 2001099220

Printed in the United States of America

06 05 04 03   6 5 4 3 2

Beaver's Pond Press, Inc.   5125 Danen's Drive
Edina, MN 55439-1465
(952) 829-8818
www.beaverspondpress.com

to order, visit *BookHouseFullfillment.com* or call 1-800-901-3480. Reseller discounts available.

Wonderful, Warm Wisdom
~ for a Lifetime

"Yesterday's the past, tomorrow's the future,
but today is a GIFT. That's why it's called
the present."

Gift List:
Table of Contents

Gifts for...

And all of it for…
Our enrichment
Through learning
Through laughter

Thank You Notes

S pecial Tribute to Bil Keane, whose Family Circus warmth, humor and comfort enters our lives and hearts like an old and treasured friend with messages of kindness and wisdom, for his generosity, encouragement and permission to use the insightful and explanatory frame of Dolly and PJ (see P. iii) which creates a context for this book as well as for living, and is truly gift to us all.

Appreciation to those named and unnamed whose insight, experience and concise observations are quoted in this book and stored in our hearts.

Deep Gratitude to Dale L. Anderson, M.D. who contributes the word "Wellderly" to refer to the wellness we experience as we "continue to have birthdays." We both represent this age-less population and provide speeches, seminars and workshops to our fellow V.P.'s (Vintage People). His energy, creativity and curiosity are inspiring!

Grateful Affection to friends for listening, reading, suggesting and supporting. You are treasures.

Recognition to Mother, Mary Lewis Williams, an energetic as well as proper "maverick" whose example liberated me to live, learn and choose.

Rejoicing to the valued minds that explore and celebrate new ideas of the aging process, refusing to accept the limits of "old ideas," of old maps for new territory!

And to each day that I am given... I cherish you.

Wellderly Wisdom:
Gifts to the Present
Directions for 'Youthage'

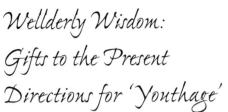

The wisdom in these pages is **precious, profound and playful gift** from those named and unnamed. It serves as "youthage" directions for LIFE! And you"re the "Youth-er!" The "**gift givers**" represent an assortment of varied personalities who share one characteristic. They have all accumulated a number of birthdays, and so are defined as "aging". You can't have one without the other! Wisdom comes too..."from the mouths of babes..." from those who haven't had as many birthdays. They're also"aging," since they will most probably have more birthdays. If they're lucky they'll continue to have them for a long time and present future generations with **nuggets of wisdom** as **treasured** as these are for us.

Most of the wisdom in this book is contained in **quotations**…about philosophy, observation, survival or just "what works!" They range from the "sublime to the ridiculous."

There are also a few **rhymes** which we might define as "gift-rap".

The process of aging…from first breath to last…wherever we are in it…is filled with **exploration** of our own as well as with **gift** from those who have already been there. They've **made discoveries** about that territory we call LIFE and have given us as gifts, comments, conclusions and ideas **to show us the way**. We may reject those gifts because of the cover, believing that something worthwhile comes only in a fresh and fashionable wrapping…no wrinkles or changes…and so impoverish and limit ourselves and our lives. But when we grasp that gift and hold it as a precious message, our lives are enriched by a **celebration of wisdom** and living that recognizes no limits.

So **accept these gifts, "youth" them well**.... Savor the nourishment....Experience the wealth...let go with the laughter...and Recognize that **YOU** are holding the **winning ticket** in the lottery of life...So

HAVE A LOVELY LIFETIME!

AND AS YOUR FIRST GIFT FOR THAT LIFETIME...

∼ NOURISHMENT ∼

Food as gift has an honored past as well as a joyful present. It's a tradition that includes elaborate dishes left in the Pyramids for Pharaohs of ancient Egypt, milk and cookies left for Santa at the fireplace on Christmas Eve, as well as the lovely box of Swiss chocolates we received as a "hostess gift" from recent dinner guests. Each represents gift for the journey, to make negotiating the terrain of living/being/breathing/aging easier. And it's the gift of the **four emotional food groups** that can **balance** and **ease your life**. You have only to seek, and....

YOU'LL find them **in this book.**

Some history, or in this case **herstory**....

My ex-neighbor had no crinkles around his eyes to tell the world that he'd smiled a lot. He hadn't... and he didn't! He **DID**, however, have a grim, firm (rigid?) and unshakable philosophy of "scarcity." In fact, he lived a really scared and sour life! "Yes, but it'll probably rain tomorrow." Or "There's no such thing as a free lunch" were his glum responses to most conversational initiatives, and statements you were guaranteed to hear at least once from him in any situation. **No awareness of gift there!**

HIS neighbor, on the other hand, (that would be **ME**) has bounteous crinkles around **HER** eyes where smiles have been, are and will be! A philosophy of **"PLENTY"** rearranges the same letters that spell s-c-a-r-e-d into **s-a-c-r-e-d,** and changes her basic life focus and philosophy to what **IS** free! Air... sunshine... the beauty of nature... friendship... thought... ideas... values... belief... heritage... **LIFE!** All free... no strings... with **responsibility**... the **ability to respond**... as the only price tag. That's one we can **ALL** pay just by being ourselves! How wonderfully and in what different ways that ability is manifested in **EVERYONE!** It's an ability honed through life's love and laughter as well as adversity... truly a **sacred trust!**

Oh yes, my crinkles have been flooded with tears and the shape of my world changed beyond any control. **We've ALL been there!** I became a widow at the age of forty six. The sudden and unexpected death of a cherished husband, treasured father and productive, world respected and beloved physician at the age of forty nine brought devastating grief. No matter what anyone says, sudden surgery is NOT painless. Brain injury to the promise in a son… loss of possessions through burglary… loss of parents to death… one final… the other with a continuing heartbeat… loss of place through moving… loss of dreams through persons… much loss in my life as is **mirrored in yours.**

And though much was irretrievably lost, **I WAS NOT!**

It was through **connection** with friends, the **stimulation** of meaningful work (to others as well as to me), the support of **faith** and the recovery of **laughter** that I experienced enough days of "survival" to re-turn my days to **"thrival!"** I never lost the first three. My friends were thoughtful, dependable and treasured **support.** My work provided the **stimulation** and reward necessary in life, and my **faith** gave me the strength and energy to move through the uncertainty and fear of lacking control. Only laughter left. I had to become intentional about re-placing it in my life. Two excellent joke books served as gateway through which my own laughter led me to a life **balanced** with the **Four Emotional Food Groups.**

And so I recommend these "food groups for the mind" to **YOU.** I **give** them to you as a guide, a **free gift of LIFE.**

Clear Nurturing

Not the sticky marshmallow kind that cloys and that serves only the giver, but the genuine, mutually caring connection and support that produce **your** growth.

Not available? Reach out; Find new friends; Do something for someone else; Breathe deeply; Call a good, positive friend.

Intellectual Stimulation

The meaningful, productive, "response to curiosity" kind...not the competitive or "pseudo" (as in "Look how smart I am!") variety.

Where to look? Try the library; Continuing Education classes at local universities, high schools, or community centers; Explore a new area of learning...one that has always interested you but is outside the usual "program"; do something creative.

Faith/Spirituality/Transcendence

The need for meaning in life which recognizes another Power in the universe. It is in recognizing Pattern and Power beyond ourselves that we experience Peace and Faith within ourselves and within the world.

Available? Freely! Perspective, respect for yourself, others and the world, and recognition of Purpose are a great beginning; Participate in a Faith Community; Pray; Meditate; Read inspirational stories; Examine your own **values** and **live** through them.

Humor

More than jokes…humor is a process, a way of looking at life and of being in the world. Think of humor as perspective, wonder, a softening, a mini-vacation from the drear of reality, a liberation, incongruity and wisdom, intimacy, authenticity, creativity, coping, an affirmation of dignity and a challenge to stereotype.

A miracle medication? Absolutely! One that's self-selected and administered, requires no prescription, supply increases with demand, and….the price is right!

So **learn from the experts**…children! They laugh 300 times a day while as serious adults we laugh 17 times a day. Become child-like, not child-ish; Watch funny videos (George Burns, Red Skelton, Jack Benny, The Marx Brothers, Abbott and Costello); Collect jokes and cartoons and make a bright yellow file for a blue day; Increase your face value, smile into the mirror; wear bright colors; Celebrate! (hey, your socks match today! Morning happened today!) Recognize the triumphs, not just the tragedies; **Play**…with ideas, words, wishes, freedom.

~

And you'll find a heaping helping of all of the Emotional Food Groups as you read this book. From the playful to the profound, the quotations, quips and "questionable quatrains"… are indeed "P's and Q's for the Mind."

Energy, curiosity, creativity, thoughts from this book as well as your own awareness are the requirements for access to this bountiful (calorie free) nourishment.

AND
"IF THE QUOTE FITS, SHARE IT!"

The Head
Thinking

What you believe the universe to be, and how you react to that belief, in everything you do, depends on what you **know**. And when that knowledge changes, for you the universe changes.

James Burke

~

For the unlearned, old age is winter; for the learned, it is the **season of the harvest**.

Hasidic Saying

~

A person's age is measured by the degree of pain felt when coming into contact with a **new idea**.

~

It's what you learn after you think you know it all that **really counts**, and that happens only with the Elixir of Age and Tincture of Time.

Most people are mirrors, reflecting the moods and emotions of the times. Few are windows, bringing light to bear on the dark corners where troubles fester. The whole **purpose of education** is to turn mirrors into windows.

Sidney Harris

Education is hanging around until you catch on.

Robert Frost

A great many people believe they are **thinking** when they are merely rearranging their prejudices.

William James

~

A person who doesn't think for him/herself doesn't think at all. Thinking can't be done by proxy.

~

All say: "How hard it is to have to die."….a strange complaint to come from the mouths of people who have had to live.

Mark Twain

~

Knowledge is proud that he has learned so much; **wisdom is humble** that he knows no more.

William Cowper

~

The fear of old age may disturb us, yet are we truly certain of growing old? Aging, after all, is **optional**.

A lot of what passes for depression is just the body or the mind saying that it **needs work.**

Youth is in the **mind**, not in the condition of your flesh.

Ginger Rogers

It's not my memory that's becoming less effective, but my **"forgettery"** that's **working really well!**

Discover ways in which you can continue the **"wonder years"** throughout your life! Not just as in "I wonder why I came into this room," or "I wonder where I put the keys/clock/cat…But as you **PLAY**…with ideas, thoughts, words…

Come up with **new definitions** for trade-marked commercial products and services as in:

Fidelity Investments: chastity belts.

Dumpster: a sleazy lawyer specializing in divorce.

Ritz crackers: wealthy rednecks.

ExLax: A listing of the shortcomings of a former spouse.

Perhaps imagination is only **intelligence having fun. Play!!**

It is the **mark of an educated mind** to be able to entertain a thought without accepting it.

Aristotle

Education is the ability to listen to almost anything without losing your temper or your self-confidence.

Robert Frost

The **happiest** person is the person who thinks the most **interesting thoughts**.

William Lyon Phelps

There are two ways to slide easily through life; believe everything or doubt everything. Both ways save you from thinking.

Thinking is like loving and dying; each of us must do it for himself.

Josiah Royce

The **human mind**, once stretched by a new idea, never regains its original shape.

William Burke

Some are wise, and some are otherwise.

It's strange how you've got to know so much before knowing how little you know.

One of the **secrets** to being wise is the art of knowing what to overlook.

I have learned throughout my life as a composer chiefly through my mistakes and pursuits of false assumptions, not by my exposure to founts of wisdom and knowledge.

Igor Stravinsky

The mind is not a vessel to be filled, but a **fire to be kindled**.

Plutarch

We can't **solve problems** with the same kind of thinking that created them in the first place.

The **greatest discovery** of my generation is that a human being can change his life by changing his attitude of mind.

William James

It's easy to come up with new **ideas**. The hard part is **letting go** of what worked for you two years ago, but will soon be out of date.

Roger Van Oech

The man who views the world at fifty the same as he did at twenty has wasted thirty years of his life.

Muhammed Ali

Only fools can be certain. It takes **wisdom** to be confused.

People with **too much time** on their hands are apt to take in bores and rumors.

Are you **living** in the present tense, or in the present, tense?

I'm not afraid of storms, for I'm **learning** how to sail my ship.

Louisa May Alcott

Is laughter good for you? Can you improve your life through humor? Funny you should ask.

~

The optimist thinks this is the best of all possible worlds. The pessimist fears this is true.

~

You can send a message around the world in 1/7 of a second; but it might take several years to move a simple idea through 1/4 inch of human skull.

~

The Heart

Feeling

It's not easy to find **happiness in ourselves**, and **it's not possible** to find it elsewhere.

Agnes Reppelier

~

In all emotional **conflicts**, the thing you find hardest to do is the one you should **do**.

Meyer Meyer

~

People become lonely because they **build** walls instead of **bridges**.

~

We may not always see eye to eye, but we can try to see **heart to heart**.

Sam Levenson

Most of the **great things in life** can be fit into one syllable: peace, love, joy, trust, home, hope.

Hardening of the **"oughteries"** ages people more quickly than hardening of the arteries.

The **supreme happiness** of life is the awareness that you are loved for yourself in spite of yourself, and that you love another because of who they are and in spite of that.

It isn't your position that makes you happy or unhappy. It's your **disposition**.

~

One person with **courage** makes a majority.

Andrew Jackson

~

People judge you by **your actions**, not your intentions. You may have a heart of gold, but so does a hard-boiled egg.

~

There are two ways to study butterflies: chase them with nets then inspect their dead bodies, or sit quietly in a garden and **watch them dance** among the flowers.

Nongnuch Bassam

~

13

Suffering is everywhere. Don't ever think it isn't. So are **miracles...everywhere!** Don't ever think they aren't!

~

The **real art** of conversation is not only to say the right thing in the right place, but to leave unsaid the wrong thing at the tempting moment.

~

To know how to grow old is the **masterwork of wisdom**, and one of the most difficult chapters in the art of living.

Henri Frederich Amiel

~

To feel that one has a **place in life** solves half the problems of contentment.

George Woodberry

~

14

Whatever/whoever angers you **controls** you.

~

There are two tragedies in life. One is not to get your **heart's desire**. The other is to get it.

George Bernard Shaw

~

Don't judge each day by the harvest you reap, but by the **seeds that you sow**.

~

One of the **advantages** of having more years is having more people to love.

~

Some people are **like popcorn**. You don't learn what they're really made of until you put the heat under them.

~

15

Courage is the art of being the only one who knows you're scared to death.

Harold Wilson

~

You are old only when your regrets about the past outnumber your dreams for the future. Otherwise, you are just **becoming**.

~

True and lasting **inner peace** can never be found in external things. It can only be found **within**. And then, once we find and nurture it within ourselves, it **radiates outward**.

~

The woods would be **very silent** if no birds sang except those that sang best.

Henry Van Dyke

~

16

The Body
Live Long

Why do we call them **goodies**, when we're told by nutritionists that they're really **baddies**.

~

Why is it whether you sit up or sit down the result is the **same?**

~

A minor operation is one performed on **someone else**.

~

Those who don't **find time** for exercise will have to find time for illness.

~

If you wish to **live long**, you must be willing to grow old.

George Lawton

~

A man too busy to take care of his health is like a carpenter too busy to take care of his tools.

~

There is a **divinity** that shapes our ends...and ends our shapes...

~

My house and I suffer from the same problems...a thinning roof, a sagging foundation, and clogged pipes.

~

It is **well documented** that for every mile you jog, you add 1 minute to your life. This enables you, at 95 years of age, to spend an additional 5 months in a nursing home at $5,000.00 per month.

~

The advantage of exercising every day is that you die **healthier**.

~

I hear that there's a **new** pill that makes you look younger...but promotes weight gain. Instead of looking sixty, you get to look like two thirty year olds.

~

Exercise early in the morning, before your brain knows what you're up to!

~

The **best reason** to take up jogging is to hear heavy breathing again.

~

If you start **walking** five miles a day when you're sixty, by the time you're 86 no one will know where you are.

Never eat more than you can lift.

The common cold can be either **positive or negative.** Sometimes the eyes have it, sometimes the nose.

The denunciation of the young is a **necessary** part of the hygiene of older people, and greatly assists the circulation of their blood.

Logan Pearsall Smith

He/She who **laughs.....lasts**.

Aging **is terrific!** Try the alternative!

Aging is **coveted** in cemeteries everywhere.

Aging rabbis tend to get gray around the temples.

When it comes to **good health**, it's not only what you eat that counts, it's what's eating you!

Age spots? I don't understand. I always thought you pretty much aged **all over!**

Secrets to staying young…live honestly, eat slowly, lie about your age; keep breathing;

The older you get the harder it is to lose weight because by that time your body has made **friends with** your fat.

Nobody grows old merely by living a number of years. People grow old by deserting their **ideas**. Years may wrinkle the skin, but to give up **interest** wrinkles the soul.

Douglas MacArthur
On his 75th birthday

How can you measure **importance**? Which breath that you draw is **un**important?

Hey

I'm **proud** of my wrinkles. The only outfit that doesn't have wrinkles is the one that hangs in the closet.

Gene Perret

The Spirit
Beyond Ourselves

We are always the **same age** inside.

Gertrude Stein

~

Discovery consists of looking at the same thing as everyone else and thinking something different.

Albert Szent-Gyorgyi

~

A **graceful and honorable** old age is the childhood of immortality.

Pindar

(Also an appropriate blessing for a newborn who has received "old" and whom we pray will have lots of it!)

~

The evening of a **well spent life** brings its lamps with it.

Joseph Joubert

Humor is a rich and versatile source of power…a **spiritual resource** very like prayer which may be the best weapon to raise against the Angel of Death, who, like the devil, cannot bear to be mocked.

Marilyn Chandler

Sometimes it's holding on that makes you **strong**. Sometimes it's letting go.

Faith is not something to grasp. It is a state to grow into.

Mohandas K. Gandhi

It takes a long time to **grow young**.

Pablo Picasso

~

You're not finished until you **decide** to give up.

~

What is **essential** is invisible to the eye.

Antoine de Saint Exupery

~

Kill off the past and we kill off the future.

~

Tragedy gives us a sense of human **courage**, comedy a sense of wild, irrational **hope**.

Peter Berger

~

25

The first and last word belong to God and therefore not to death but to **life**, not to sorrow but **joy**, not to weeping but **laughter**.

Conrad Hyers

As for me, I know of nothing else but **miracles**.

Walt Whitman

We are not human beings trying to be spiritual. We are **spiritual beings** trying to be human.

Jacquelyn Small

No coward soul is mine,
No trembler in the world's storm-troubled
   sphere:
I see Heaven's glories shine,
And faith shines equal, arming me from
   fear.

                          Emily Bronte

—and be alive this day, as though it were
not first or last, just best.

27

The World
Legacy

What we do for ourselves dies with us. What we do for others and the world remains and is **immortal**.

Albert Pine

~

It's not how old you are that **counts**, but how you are old.

~

Life is like a play…it's not the length that counts, but the **performance**.

~

There is **no such thing** in anyone's life as an unimportant day.

~

Age isn't **important** unless you're a cheese.

We must **become** the change we want to see.

Mohandas K. Gandhi

To **change** and to **improve** are two different things.

To **change** and to **improve** are two different things.

Everything has its beauty, but not everyone sees it.

Confucius

Almost anything you do will be insignificant, but it is **important** that you do it.

Mohandas K. Gandhi

If you think you can, **you're right**. If you think you can't, **you're right**.

~

Character is defined by **what you are willing to do when the spotlight has been turned off**, the applause has died down and no one is around to give you the credit.

Ann Landers

~

Disney went broke seven times **believing** that a mouse could be a movie star.

~

Between two evils, I always choose the one I have never tried before.

Mae West

~

Loyalty to petrified opinion never yet broke a chain or freed a human **soul**.

Mark Twain

Even if you're on the **right track**, you'll get run over if you just sit there.

Will Rogers

Remember that the **faith that moves mountains** always carries a pick.

Be a fountain, not a drain.

Ourselves

Personal

Your best **dreams** may not come true. Fortunately, neither will your worst dreams.

R.A. Newman

When a man is **wrapped up** in himself he makes a pretty small package.

John Ruskin

Age is **no cause** for veneration. An old crocodile is still a menace and an old crow sings not like a nightingale.

Life is like a ten-speed bike. Most of us have gears we never use.

Charles Schultz

The way I see it, if you want the **rainbow**, you gotta put up with the rain.

Dolly Parton

Never wave to your friends at an auction.

Perfection has no completion date.

If you try to fail and **succeed**, which have you done?

A pessimist is a person who mourns the future.

Isabelle C. Dickson

34

Live out of your **imagination**, not your history.

Stephen R. Covey

Life is like a piano...**upright and grand**...and what you get out of it depends largely on how you **play** it.

Any idiot can face a crisis, it's this **day-to-day** living that wears you out.

Anton Chekhov

Live each day as though it were your first.
YOU'RE RIGHT!
Live each day as though it were your last.
Someday you'll BE right!

35

You can't tell how **deep** a puddle is until you step in it.

Lying makes a problem part of the future; **truth** makes a problem a part of the past.

Imagination was given to man to compensate him for what he is not; and a **sense of humor** was provided to console him for what he is.

Oscar Wilde

The price of **freedom** is that we must put up with a good deal of rubbish.

We get "age" the moment we're born! That's when we start to experience, learn about and **do it!** We **spend our lives** learning how to age. We discover how to **solve problems**, to adopt and to live our

36

values, recognize our own **significance and uniqueness**, learn how to **interact** with others, to **care for** our world, and to **contribute** to our own lives as well as to those of others. So go for it!

~

Wish not so much to live long as to **live well**, and both may be granted.

~

The gift of **happiness** belongs to those who unwrap it.

~

Good sound reasons and reasons that sound good are not the same thing.

~

How old **would you be** if you didn't know how old you was?

Satchel Page

~

Ever notice how everyone wants to go to **Heaven**, but no one wants to die?

Now that you know your way around, you may not feel like going.

It's better to be old and bent than old and broke.

When you're through changing...you're through!

If we **Expire** when we die, shouldn't we **Inspire** while we live?

You cannot "pursue happiness". It's an abstraction. **Happiness is the byproduct** of being involved in that most rewarding of activities…**LIFE!**

A laugh is a **smile that has burst!** "Smiles bursting in air" should be a line in our personal anthem!

Choose carefully the history you write today.

Get into the habit of getting out of the habit!

The trick is **growing up** AND **growing older** without growing old.

39

All the Constitution guarantees is the **PURSUIT** of happiness. You'll have to catch up with it yourself.

~

CHOOSE! Don't succumb to "hardening of the 'oughteries'"

~

Success is getting what you want. **Happiness** is wanting what you get.

~

Did you finally find the **courage** to face the music...and find that it's in surround sound?

~

If you can't grow old gracefully...**do it any way you can.**

~

Life is a lot more **fun** if you think of dust as a noun instead of a verb.

~

People will accept your ideas more **readily** if you tell them that Benjamin Franklin said it first.

~

The worried man who can manage a **smile** will unnerve his enemies more than the cowering wreck or the blustering blow-hard.

~

The caterpillar's end is the butterfly's **beginning**.

~

Don't think you can **use up** calories by jumping to conclusions, climbing the walls, or pushing your luck! That's no diet, and anyway, you're just apt to get hurt.

~

Integrity is doing the right thing even if nobody is watching.

~

There's hardly a person alive who couldn't retire **comfortably** in his/her old age if they could sell their experience for what it cost them!

~

Life is a fatal adventure. It can have only one end. So why not make it as **exciting, worthwhile and creative as possible!**

~

Growing old is something you do if you're **lucky**.

Groucho Marx

~

On the banister of life **may you find** no splinters.

~

Spiritual eyesight **improves** as physical eyesight declines.

~

Very few people do anything creative beyond the age of 35. **The reason** is that very few people do anything creative before the age of 35.

Joel Hildebrand

~

What then is the right way to live? Life should be lived as **play**.

Plato

~

An optimist **laughs** to forget; A pessimist forgets to laugh.

~

Life is **wonderful**. Without it you're dead.

Red Skelton

Humor is not a trick, not jokes. Humor is a presence in the world and **shines on everyone.**

Garrison Keillor

The secret of eternal youth is arrested development.

Stress is something you get from climbing molehills.

Others

Connection

Character is like a tree and **reputation** is like its shadow. The shadow is what we think of it. The tree is the real thing.

Abe Lincoln

~

The faults of others are like the headlights on an automobile. They only **SEEM** more glaring than our own.

~

What is hateful to you, do not to your fellow man. That is the **entire law**; all the rest is commentary.

The Talmud

~

Do not wrong or hate your neighbor for it is not he that you wrong but **yourself**.

Native American Proverb

No matter what goes wrong, there is always somebody who **knew it would**.

The only thing some people do for themselves is feel sorry, and even then they like **help**.

Some people know a lot more than they're willing to tell. Unfortunately, the **reverse** is also true.

Sensible people are easily recognized. Either they express agreement with our opinions, or admiration for our work.

Happiness never decreases by being shared.

~

Funny thing about life; if you refuse to accept nothing but the best, **you very often get it.**

Somerset Maugham

~

Some people **cause happiness** whenever they come, others whenever they go.

~

We don't have much choice in how we're going to die, or when. We **CAN** decide how we're going to **LIVE.**

~

The injuries we do and those we suffer are **seldom** weighed in the **same scale.**

Aesop

~

We may not have all come over in the same ship…but we're all in **the same boat**.

Bernard Baruch

~

There are two kinds of **friends**; those who are around when you need them, and those who are around when they need you.

~

An egomaniac is a self-made person who **insists** on giving you the recipe.

~

A **smile** is the shortest distance between two people.

~

48

Our Face (Sense of Humor)
"Smile Awhile" or "Chuckle Luck"

Things aren't like they used to be….and they **never were!**

~

Improve your face value…**smile!**

~

Aging is when you **do your part** and keep the top of the television clear of all musical instruments because there's enough sax and violins on television already!

~

Beware! A person who has always been the productive, energetic sort, will have trouble adjusting to a life of leisure. It could take as long as **four minutes** before all desire to ever work "like that" again disappears and an **enthusiasm** for **what's now** and **what's next** takes it's place!

∼

"You don't know what hard work is! Why, when I was your age I was a lot **younger** than you and I was working 18 hours a day!"

∼

Wrinkles merely indicate where **smiles** have been.

∼

Helpful hints aren't.

∼

Confidence is when you can tell the salesman who calls that you're really not interested in aluminum siding, but that you're so glad that he called so you can tell him about the most recent operation you had in YOUR side.

∼

Birthdays are like cheap underwear, they tend to creep up on you.

~

The **fastest growing thing** in nature is a fish....from the time you catch it until you tell somebody about it.

~

Too often people who are bored become members of the **meddle class**.

~

As affections mature, tall, dark and handsome is replaced by **short, bald and hassome.**

~

Are you on the critical list? Critical of neighbors, others, the food, "teenagers", "nowadays"?

~

When your **dreams** turn to dust, vacuum.

If life were **fair**, people would occasionally fly over pigeons.

Hey, this **IS** the other side and the grass **IS** greener.

PMA (Positive Mental Attitude)…Don't leave home without it!

Sleeping at the wheel is another good way not to grow old.

Think of your face as a **beautiful poem**. You can't decide which line you like the best.

On receiving a **distinguished service award:** "I don't deserve this. But then, I have arthritis and I don't deserve that either!"

~

You can't have **everything,** where would you put it?

~

There's something **crazy** in the notion that remaining alive is the worst thing that could possibly happen to you!

~

Do you ever feel like your **reality check** bounced?

~

Why fret and rush? **Consider the dia- mond.** It was once just a lump of coal under pressure.

~

53

Warning. Dates on calendar are **closer than they appear.**

~

Why, when you're dog tired, do you take a cat nap?

~

All this talk about low fat, low fat. They're talking about me just because I'm short!

~

My Mother was a genius in the kitchen…especially with leftovers. She was **so skilled** that no one ever remembered the original meal!

~

Housework can't kill you, but why take a **chance?**

Phyllis Diller

~

54

Experience is like money. Just when you think you've had enough, something happens and you wish you'd had more.

Laughter, like the best gasoline, helps take the knocks out…of life.

Childhood is that wonderful time when all you needed to do to lose weight was to take a bath.

When we were **promised** "Lo, I am with you always" did that refer to our golf score, our weight or our age?

Be **proud** of the candles on your cake. They're a great heat source.

Worrying about the past is like trying to make birth control pills retroactive.

~

Tact is like air in your automobile tires. Without it, driving through life is pretty tough.

~

There's one thing about being bald. It's **neat.**

~

Of all the things you wear, **expression** is the most important.

~

I started out with nothing and **still have** most of it left.

~

He doesn't have ulcers, but he **is** a carrier.

~

You may find that whine doesn't go with what is being served.

Where am I **going?** And why am I in a handbasket?

Indigestion is **what you get** when a square meal won't fit into a round stomach.

Just think, in a few years Barney will be motor oil.

Learn from the politician. When you throw dirt at those you oppose, all you do is lose ground.

Everybody is a moon, and has a dark side which they never show to anybody.

Mark Twain

You start out with a **bag full of luck** and an empty bag of experience. The trick is to fill the bag of experience before emptying the bag of luck.

Our Understanding

Purpose

Life is full of obstacle illusions.

~

There are no hopeless situations, there are only people who have grown helpless about them.

~

Forgiveness is not an occasional act, it's a permanent **attitude**.

~

Resolve to be **tender** with the young, **compassionate** with the aged, **sympathetic** with the striving, and **tolerant** of the weak and the wrong. Sometime in life you've been all those things.

~

We make a living by what we **get**. We make a life by what we **give**.

Norman McEwan

~

To affect the quality of the days, that is the **highest** of acts.

Henry David Thoreau

~

There are takers and givers in life. The takers may eat better but the **givers sleep better**.

~

The **most valuable gift** you can give another at any age is a good example.

~

Worry if you must, but about somebody besides yourself! You may have spent your **LIFE** worrying and you've developed it into an art form! Use this talent to worry about **others** and **make the world a better**

place. But don't just worry, **DO** something and let worry be a **springboard** to action rather than a rocking chair that moves a lot but goes nowhere!

Stay away from the **wisdom** that does not cry, the **philosophy** that does not laugh, and the **greatness** that does not bow before children.

Change your "guilt-edged" life to one that is truly **gilt-edged**. Recognize the silver lining.

I am only one, but I am one
I can't do everything
But I can do **something**.
And what I can do I ought to do
And what I ought to do
By the grace of God, I will do.

Anonymous

Old age is like everything else. To make a **success** of it, you've got to **start young**.

~

If you wish to **live long**, you must be willing to grow old.

George Lawton

~

Anyone who still **expects to grow** is young…no matter what the calendar says!

~

The trouble with the **future** is that it's not what it used to be.

Those Days
Survive and Thrive!

The dead bird does not leave the nest.

Winston Churchill
(on being advised that his fly was open.)

~

You're not as young as you used to be. But you're not as old as you're going to be. So **watch it!**

Irish Toast

~

Never insult an alligator until **after** you've crossed the river.

Cordell Hull

~

They say **such nice things** about people at their funerals that it makes me sad to realize that I'm going to miss mine by just a few days.

Garrison Keillor

~

You can't turn back the clock, but you can certainly make sure you **wind it!**

~

Think lucky. If you fall in a pond, check your hip pocket for fish.

Darrell Royal

~

Never get into a battle of wits without ammunition.

~

I find TV very **educational**. When my husband turns it on, I read a book.

~

If you think that "life's just not worth living," ask yourself **what else** you'd do with it.

~

If everything seems to be coming your
way, you may be in the wrong lane.

~

If it weren't for the **last minute**, nothing
would get done.

~

65 is a Speed Limit…not an age limit

~

The **secret** of **getting ahead** is getting
started.

~

You can add life to your years…and even years to your life by…

Discovering that the IRS owes you money

Hearing the plumber say "my treat"

Finding your luggage on the airline carousel

Realizing that the neighbor's dog has spared your geraniums

Awakening in the morning

Realizing that your glasses were on your face all the time and that the lenses are just really clean

No longer resenting taxes and beginning to think of them as a cover charge for life.

Referring to those increasing configurations around your eyes not as wrinkles…but proudly calling them "crinkles"

Acknowledging that the late bird has it all over the early bird because getting sleep is sure better than getting worms!

To whom it may concern:

I am hereby **officially tendering my resignation as an adult in order to accept the responsibilities of a six year old.**

- I want to think M&M's are **better than money** because you can eat them.
- I long for the days when life was **simple**, when all you knew were your colors; the addition tables, and simple nursery rhymes but it didn't bother you because you didn't know what you didn't know and you didn't care.
- I want to be happy because I don't know what should make me upset.
- I want to think the world is **fair** and everyone is honest and good.
- I want to believe that anything is **possible**.

Sometime, while I was maturing, I learned too much. I learned of nuclear weapons, prejudice, starving and abused kids, unhappy marriages, illness, pain and mortality.

I want to be six again...**but just for awhile.**

There's no time like the **pleasant**.

To **maintain perspective** it's important to remember that you'll encounter people with more dollars than sense.

If you are walking on thin ice, you might as well dance!

Our Perspective
Balance

The **difference** between genius and stupidity is that genius has its limits.

~

Doing nothing is the **most tiring work in the world.** You can't rest and you can't quit.

~

Maturity is realizing that household chores are just avoidable annoyances.

~

Retirement is when a **"power breakfast"** means you left the toaster plugged in.

~

Fear of becoming a has-been, keeps some people from being anything at all.

Develop the attitude of **"What's next?"**!

Happiness comes into our lives through doors we don't even remember leaving open.

Rose Lane

Life is **lived more fully** when you do it like you pick raspberries. You miss a lot if you approach it from only one angle.

Everything has been thought of before but the problem is to think of it **again**.

Goethe

If they're running you out of town, get in front and pretend it's a **parade.**

It is not **the same** to talk of bulls as to be in the bullring.

One of the **delights** known to age, and beyond the grasp of youth, is that of Not Going.

Our problems, held too close to our vision, will hide the universe and its **won- ders** as well as the **solutions** to those problems!

If you think you're a person of **influence**, try ordering around someone else's dog.

Laughter rises out of tragedy **when you need it the most** and **rewards** you for your courage.

Erma Bombeck

Work and play are two words used to describe the **same thing** under different conditions.

Mark Twain

Worry is like a rocking chair. It'll give you something to do, but it won't get you anywhere.

Poverty consists not in the decrease of one' possessions, but in the **increase** of one's greed.

Plato

There are **two ways to be rich**. One is to have a lot of money, the other is to have few needs.

William Sloane Coffin

Trouble is only **opportunity in work clothes.**

Henry J. Kaiser

Aging is **optional**…try arsenic.

If age is the price we pay for maturity, we'll pay the highest one possible!

I don't understand why I have to grow old before somebody will tell me that I look **young for my age.**

What Mother Nature **giveth**; Father Time **taketh** away.

~

Life shrinks or expands in proportion to one's **courage**.

~

Happiness isn't getting what you want, but **wanting what you get**. Just think of all the things that you don't want that you don't get!

~

Ever notice that when your **cup runneth over**, someone bumpeth your elbow?

~

Like cheese and wine, we **ripen** into **desirable maturity**.

~

74

True perspective of one's importance comes from having a dog that will worship you and a cat that will ignore you.

~

Do not resist growing old. Many are denied the **privilege**!

Irish Toast

~

You can complain because rose bushes have thorns, or you can **rejoice** because thorn bushes have roses! It's all in how you look at things.

~

When you've raised your children, stop raising them!

~

If you find yourself in a hole, the **first thing to do** is stop digging.

~

75

Being bitten to death by ducks is a bit like being stoned to death with popcorn.

~

The **best things in life** aren't things.

~

Life is a stairway, not an escalator. You have to move up under **your own power.**

~

You can't leave **footprints** in the sand of time by sitting down.

~

On being asked about the status of his eyesight as he celebrated his 87th birthday, J.C. Penney replied: "My eyesight isn't as keen as it was, but my **vision** has never been better!"

(Shared by Ed Scannell and included here with his permission)

~

Our Present
Gift Now

The main pathology of later years, is our idea of later years.

I can't imagine a **wise** old person who can't **laugh**.

Erik H. Erikson

The greatest mistake in life is to do nothing because you can only do a little. **Do what you can.**

I am not afraid of tomorrow, for I have seen yesterday and **I love today.**

William Allen White

The best way to make your **dreams come true** is to wake up.

~

Don't cry because it's over. **Rejoice** because it happened!

~

Maturity brings the ability to admire **patience** in the driver in front of you as well as the driver behind you.

~

Death is more universal than life. Everyone dies, but not everyone **lives.**

~

Time is the **most precious gift** in our possession, for it is the most irrevocable.

Dietrich Bonhoeffer

~

Time is very **versatile**. It marches on, heals all wounds, flies, will tell, and runs out.

~

It's not so much how busy you are, but **how you are busy**. The bee is praised, the mosquito is swatted.

Marie O'Connor

He who has a **"why"** to live, can bear with almost any "how".

Nietzche

If you cannot **find the truth** right where you are, where else do you expect to find it?

Life is a horse, and either you ride it or it rides you.

You don't get to choose how you're going to die, or when, just **how you live!**

Life is a continuous **process** of getting used to things we hadn't expected.

We shouldn't put off until tomorrow what we can do today, because if we **enjoy it today** we can **do it again tomorrow**.

If I have a heart condition and you operate on my foot, the problem remains.

Normal day, let me be aware of the **treasure** you are. Let me learn from you, love you, savor you, bless you before you depart. Let me not pass you by in quest of some rare and perfect tomorrow. Let me **hold you** while I may, for it will not always be so.

Mary Jean Irion

And the poet speaks of **success**…
>To **laugh** often and much…
>To win the **respect** of intelligent people and the **affection** of children…
>To earn the **appreciation** of honest critics and **endure** the betrayal of false friends…
>To **appreciate** beauty…
>To find the **best** in others…
>To leave the world a bit **better**, whether by a healthy child, a garden patch, or a redeemed social condition…
>To know even **one life** has breathed easier because you have lived…
>**This is to have succeeded.**

Our Future

Wings

Life is like a bank account. You get out what you put in and experience is the interest we earn in the process.

~

The **future** is no more uncertain than the present.

Walt Whitman

~

Thousands of candles can be **lighted** from a **single candle**, and the life of the candle will not be shortened.

Buddha

When those with more "old" read the Bible, are they "cramming for finals"?

~

Children are a **message** we send to a time we will not see.

~

Keep a green tree in your **heart** and perhaps the **singing bird** will come.

Chinese Proverb

~

Worry is the interest we pay on trouble before it's due.

~

No one can walk backward into the **future**.

Joseph Hergesheimer

~

Our **interest** must be in the future, because that's where we'll spend the rest of our lives. Our **actions** must be in the present, for that's where we can effect change.

One generation plants the trees;
Another gets the **shade**.

Chinese Proverb

Lord, make my words **sweet and tender**, for tomorrow I may have to eat them.

My **direction** is **more important** than my speed.

It seems we spend half our life trying to find something to do with the time we have rushed through life trying to save.

Will Rogers

Teaching is the greatest act of optimism.

Colleen Wilcox

You can count how many **seeds** are in the apple, but not how many **apples** are in the seed.

Ken Kersey

Our Past

Roots

Without **courage, vision and faith**, Michaelangelo would have painted the Sistine floor.

Life can only be understood backwards, but it must be lived forwards.

Soren Kirkagaard

Fear of becoming a has-been prevents some people from becoming anything.

Experience is simply the name we give our mistakes.

Oscar Wilde

Results! Why, man, I've gotten a lot of results. I know several thousand things that won't work.

Thomas A. Edison

The probability that we may fail in the struggle ought not to deter us from the support of **a cause we believe to be just.**

Abe Lincoln

You're not finished until you decide to give up.

It's **better** to wear out than rust out.

If you lack what you need, then **use** what you've got!

Many people go through life running from something that isn't after them.

God gave us burdens, also **shoulders**.

Yiddish Proverb

Remembering makes life pleasurable, but forgetting makes it **possible**.

The opposite of success isn't trying, it's **getting started**.

The greatest **sacrament** that survival administers is **gratitude**.

When you drink the water, remember the spring.

Aging seems to be the only available way to live a long life.

Gift Rap
Rhymes for our Times

Star Stuff

Wrinkles, wrinkles on my face,
How I wonder at your place
Out in front for all to see
Not on my feet, tucked under me.
But all the wrinkles on my phiz
Tell the world I WAS and IS!

Annie Glasgow

Mirror Mirror, On the Walk

Mirror, mirror on the walk,
I'm sorry I dropped you
But it was such a shock
To gaze into your reflective surface
And see MY FACE
It made me *nerface*!
To discover my skin filled with folds,
pleats and wrinkles
While around my eyes are bounteous
crinkles!
I won't mention assorted gathers and sags
And under my eyes…they're not MONEY
BAGS!

Now I know that my visage isn't the best
But when did it get to be so "unpressed"?
And still, it's MY FACE and it's wonder-
fully "lived in".
I've EARNED those expressions…from
forehead to chin.

It's been with me faithfully,
recorded my life
From gaiety and joy to
suffering and strife.
It's unique, it's beautiful,
it's totally MINE,
Every sag, dimple, wrinkle
and every etched line!

It's really terrific, this face I've been given,
I've earned all that "doodling", it means
I've been livin'!
I'm still sad, mirror, that you are bro-
ken...but also glad that you have spoken
Of the value, uniqueness, the wonder
that's me,
For when I look next I'll remember this
text
And TREASURE the face that I see!

Annie Glasgow

Universal Truths

When you're born you draw your first
breath.
And when you stop breathing, that's
called death.
And in between we breathe and age
That's called living.
It's ALL the rage!

Annie Glasgow

Lines on Turning Forty

I have a bone to pick with Fate.
Come here and tell me, girlie,
Do you think my mind is maturing late,
Or simply rotted early?

Ogden Nash

Get Ready, Get Set, Grow!

When your crinkles turn to wrinkles and
your wrinkles turn to seams;
When your nicely rounded bottom is a
widely flattened beam;
When you see your outsides changing
while your insides stay the same
So the "old act" won't be your pattern;
Keep on growing! That's the game!

Annie Glasgow

To Be

I'd like to be a "could be" if I could not
be an "are"
For a "could be" is a "would be" with a
chance of reaching par.
I'd rather be a "has been" that a "might
have been" by far
For a "might have been" has never been,
but a "has been" was an "are".)

Lines on Becoming Wellderly or
They're Not ALL on My Face

Well here I've arrived (somewhat
helterdly skelterdly)
At the time when I celebrate being
Wellderly!
I've collected birthdays, one by one
And I won't refuse any, it's just not done!
The years have been tender,
sometimes they've been tough,
But however they've happened
there've been enough
To include me as one of the favored,
the lucky,
The Wonderful Wellderly, and that's
just ducky!
Oh yes, Life has used me and I certainly
know it,
I look it, I feel it, but still think I owe it
For the glory, the splendor, the joy that
it's given,
I rejoice in it, savor it, and want to
keep livin'!

Annie Glasgow

*This Certificate
entitles bearer to CHOOSE
as many of the statements
from this book which he/she
finds most meaningful,
COMBINE them with
his/her own UNIQUE philosophy, experience and talents,
and RECOGNIZE the
IMPORTANCE of
herself/himself, of each day,
and of BEING ALIVE!"*

Gift Givers

A. Nony Mouse
Aesop
Louis May Alcott
Muhammed Ali
Henri Frederich Amiel
Aristotle
Joan Baez
Bernard Baruch
Nongnuch Bassam
Peter Berger
Erma Bombeck
Dietrich Bonhoeffer
Emily Bronte
Buddha
James Burke
Marilyn Chandler
Anton Checkov
Winston Churchill
William Sloane Coffin

Confucious
Stephen R. Covey
William Cowper
Isabelle C. Dickson
Phyllis Diller
Thomas Edison
Erik H. Erikson
Robert Frost
Mohandas K. Gandhi
Maryann Glasgow
Goethe
Sidney Harris
Joel Heidelbrand
Cordell Hull
Conrad Hyers
Mary Jean Irion
Andrew Jackson
William James
Joseph Joubert
Henry J. Kaiser
Garrison Keillor
Soren Kirkagaard
Ann Landers

Rose Lane
George Lawton
Mary Jean LeTendre
Sam Levenson
Abraham Lincoln
Douglas MacArthur
Groucho Marx
Somerset Maugham
Norman McEwan
Meyer Meyer
Ogden Nash
R.A. Newman
Nietzche
Marie O'Connor
Satchel Page
Dolly Parton
J.C. Penney
Gene Perret
Pablo Picasso
Albert Pine
Plato
William Lyon Phelphs
Plutarch

Pindar
Agnes Reppelier
Ginger Rogers
Will Rogers
Darrel Royal
Josiah Royce
John Ruskin
Antoine de Saint-Exupery
Charles Schultz
George Bernard Shaw
Jacquelyn Small
Logan Pearsall Smith
Gertrude Stein
Igor Stravinsky
Albert Szent-Gyorgyi
Henry David Thoreau
Mark Twain
Henry Van Dyke
Roger VanOech
Mae West
William Allen White
Walt Whitman
Colleen Wilcox

Harold Wilson
Oscar Wilde
George Woodberry

About the Author

Maryann "Annie" Glasgow, a Professional Speaker as well as a Psychotherapist, has enjoyed many birthdays and looks forward to many more! She has worked with all ages of "personhood" from abused children to depressed adults to those in the "stressed out" workforce, to the "wellderly" of our society. She playfully presents a new concept of age that serves as an inspiration and adjunct to our own health self-care. An advocate of "Planned Personhood," she recommends "consulting the experts" as we chart this adventure we call Living.

This book represents the fruit of many lives, all thoroughly lived by the "experts" (those who have joyfully celebrated MANY birthdays) included.

Dale L. Anderson, M.D. A physician for over 40 years, as well as a Professional Speaker, he created the exciting and elegantly simple synthesis of the performing arts and health that are the subject of his books *Act Now* and *Never Act Your Age*. His curiosity and enthusiasm represent a wonderful model of "Wellderly" living and continued contribution and creativity.